Find your own light through challenges of life

Motivational Poems

Kiane Young

DEDICATION

Firstly, I need to honor that my higher power comes from a place only I would ever really understand. Without a belief of something greater than myself I honestly am not sure I would have pushed through so many devastating obstacles with such integrity.

My mom, may she continue to rest in peace. Although we didn't have the healthiest relationship, she always found a way to encourage me to pursue my goals. Watching her overcome a long painful drug and alcohol addiction inspired me and taught me that all things are possible if you truly want change.

Most importantly my three amazing kids- Quazori, Azari and Skye'. You are the driving force in all that I do. When I look at each and every one of you my heart fills with so much love and joy. As I listen to you speak on your own goals and aspirations It makes me realize that I have definitely been serving my true purpose as your mother. I couldn't be more grateful, my higher power gifted you to me and you are very unique individuals. I am so proud of all of you.

CONTENTS

ACKNOWLEDGMENTS

To all of you who have ever planted a seed in my life by showing genuine love and support always. Never letting me give up with your constant reminders of how far I have come along my journey. There are too many to name but you know who you are. Just know, as I accomplish all that I am destined to be in this lifetime is a reflection of you.

To all of my clients that I have worked with over the years. It has been a privilege to work with you, thank you for trusting me to guide you, for keeping the faith, healing and staying the course. Watching you evolve right before my eyes is most rewarding. You have contributed to this book in ways that you perhaps may not even realize. Remember, always reignite your flame in life!

Much appreciation to the awesome Amazon Pro Hub Publishing team for your outstanding assistance with this project. Your dedication, efficiency and personable approach is unmatched.

To my readers who are feeling broken, as though all is lost and feel there is nowhere to turn, let me remind you with these poems that there is always forward movement and energy is forever flowing. Choose you and live as if you are already abundant, it is all about perception, the energy that you invest into your situation will reflect on your outcomes. Bless you all!
~Kiane Young

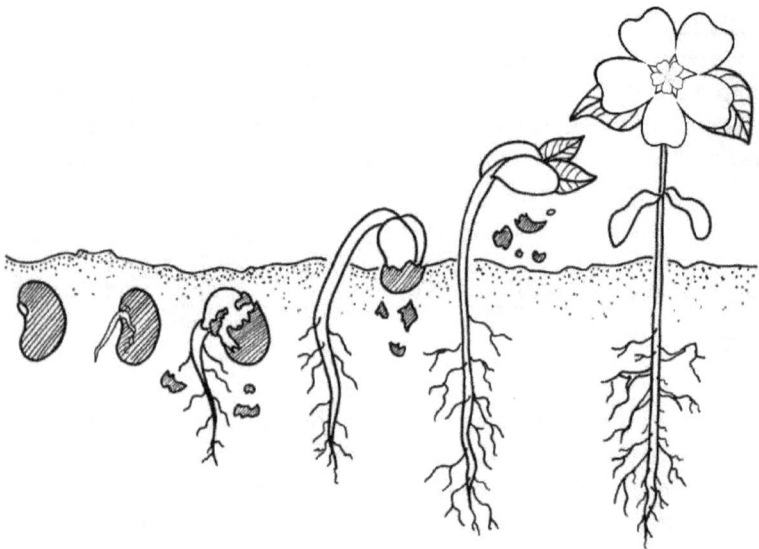

The Process

I am just a seed, planted in rich soil.
Hoping my gardener remains loyal.

Needing to be bathed in warmth.
Showered with blessings, embracing the lessons.

Taking a while to sprout, all the others are
blooming.
Is it just me, is it something I'm not doing?

I guess it's not my season.
All things happen in time, for no real reason.

Excited to see how I develop, from stem to the top.
I want to stand firm and my nutrients help a lot.
So many have curved, I feel it non-stop.

The day is here, my shell busted.
All because I trusted.

Months went by. I've completely sprouted.
Now I know if all else fails, never to doubt it.

Emperor Energy

You are an Emperor. It's time to embrace your
power.
Every time you resist change, life crumbles. You
experience a crushed tower.

Learn the lessons, nothing but growth, the wounds
are so deep.
Peel back the layers as you start to seek.

Once you find your true being.
Then you can have your new beginning.

Heal your childhood trauma, forgive the person.
Who hurt you, your father, or mama? It may be
none.
Whatever is causing you a block?
Crush it like a monster truck.
All it takes to get unstuck.

An Emperor is the King of all Kings.
Nothing can stop his mission or clip his wings.

A magical being, passionate toward his lover.
Business savvy, extremely clever.

Always decisive, sure of himself as he stands tall.
This is required so that he doesn't fall.
Now, go on and claim it all!

Message from a Bird

Wings cannot always be dependable. Make good use
of them when you're strong.
Flap them hard, no matter how short or long.

Wings cannot always be dependable. Take chances
when opportunities come.
Don't fear when your heart skips a beat, to get the
chance you've already won!

Wings cannot always be dependable. So fly in
flocks, confide in others, avoid the vultures.
Not too low, watch out the tree! You just lost
feathers.

Wings cannot always be dependable. Never take on
too much to handle, fly through the storm.
Relax your wings, accept the new norm.

Wings cannot always be dependable. Embrace the
blue sky, bright sun sitting high.
Learn through the journey! When you feel stuck, no
need to ask why?
Let go and remember, just because you have wings
doesn't mean you can fly.

Empress Energy

You are an Empress, stand your ground, never feel
hopeless.
Be in control of your own destiny, only do what
you can.
The rest will be what it's supposed to be.
Keep close eyes on your circle, untrustworthy
people, not all of them are neutral.

As you stand in your power, the energy will shift.
Like a storm in the night, in such a swift.
Your path now clear, obstacles withered in the air,
time to push on.
Feeling abundant, don't let fear make you too
stubborn.

As an empress, you attract happiness.
Such a beautiful soul, spiritual healer, energy so
fresh.
Whenever in your presence, blinded by your light.
You need to take a step back, so confident, shining
bright.

Intimidating to approach at times.
You're really just focused on your grind, release the
dark shadows.
Now you see forward motion, success.
Elevation, ambition, all that flows.

Mama RIP
4/20/59 - 12/31/19

Happy Birthday mama, my heart weighs heavy,
today and every day.
As you're in my thoughts, my mind ponders.
So many questions unanswered.

However, those three-hour conversations, the
clarity in understanding our differences.
Brought closure and healing to our past
experiences.

Within your last six months on earth, I got to know
the real you, more than I ever have since birth.
Ooh, f*** this hurts so much, deep breaths I must
take, constant stops.

Trying to get through my goals as we discussed.
I realize the armor you wore was polished in tough
love.
The lessons you learned came from the father
above.

Your memory will forever linger especially the visits
in my dreams.
One of the strongest women I've ever seen, today is
your day to be celebrated, I love you, Queen!

High Vibes

It's something about that high vibe, the feeling of
completeness, no agony.
Floating without a care in the world, no fake vibe,
fugazi!
It's something about that high vibe! Can't deal with
the bullshit, just wanting to quit!
Can't do that either, stop complaining, or deal with
it.

Now look at this mess. Ok lesson learned, time to
pick up the pieces, still blessed, no stress!
It's something about that high vibe, driving force,
manifestation. Now look at your dreams come into
fruition.

High vibes do go up and down.
There's no need to panic, no need to frown.
The cycle of life keeps you on your grind.
Now chin up, toast to that! Juice or wine?

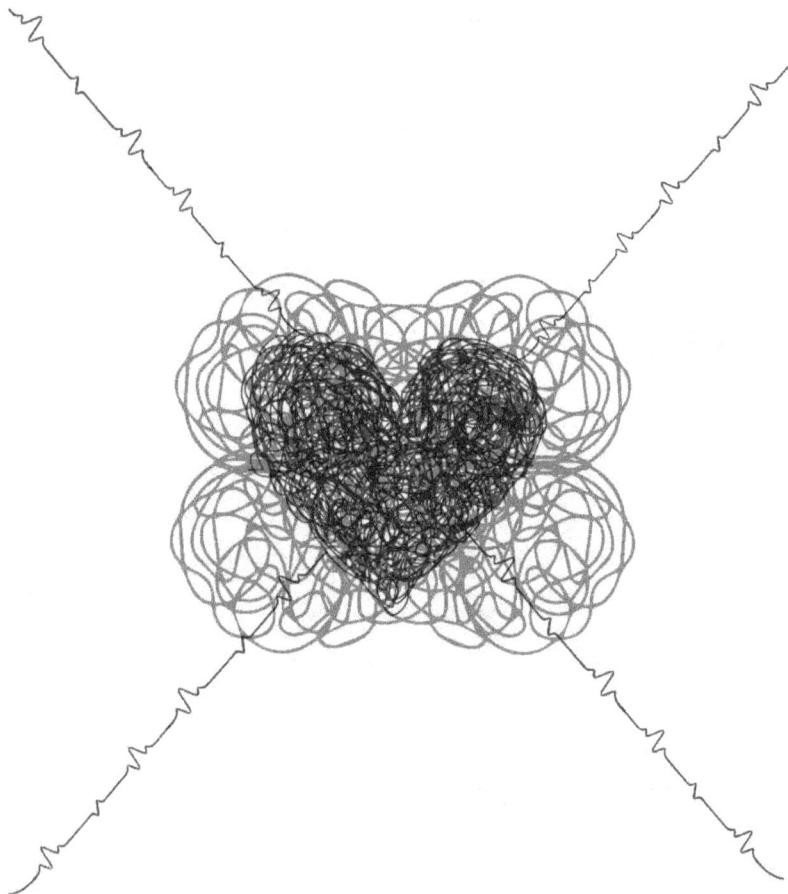

Love in Chaos

All I ever wanted was to be loved, crying.
Praying to my father above, please give me a sign.
Losing control, losing my mind.
I'm just a child, fights and arguments, so much
dysfunction, is this a home, or out in the wild.

Always wondered, where my love for nature came
from?
Just loved the outdoors, the safest place to run.
Police bust in, oh no! Is that a dog? Frozen in
silence, so confused by it all.
Mom just says stand behind the wall.

It's only a fight, why the dogs? Cop shouts out,
"Find the drugs". Man what a day of horror, didn't
know days like this would turn me into a warrior.
As the tears flow down my face, cops take notes to
build their case.
Same thing time and time again, cherish the good
times, another fight coming, don't know when.

No matter how dysfunctional, in my eyes you were
exceptional. All I wanted was love.
Didn't realize I Always had it from my father above.

Illusions

Confusion is nothing but an illusion, needing clarity,
not insecurity.
Time to go within, listen to your intuition, what
does it say? It's time to pray.

The feeling is so intense, straddling this fence, not
knowing which side is best.
I'm exhausted, time to rest, heart pounding out of
my chest.

New day, letting go of yesterday, exercise seems
wise.
I continue to fall, just like phoenix, I rise.

Confusion is nothing but an illusion, really
surrounded by good people, I'm fruitful.
Rich not only in wealth, a beautiful soul brings good
mental health.

Changes are so rewarding, stay the course, stop worrying. Now look, you graduated, stay elevated. Only up from here, my dear!
You're amazing, fascinating, there is no one like you anywhere.

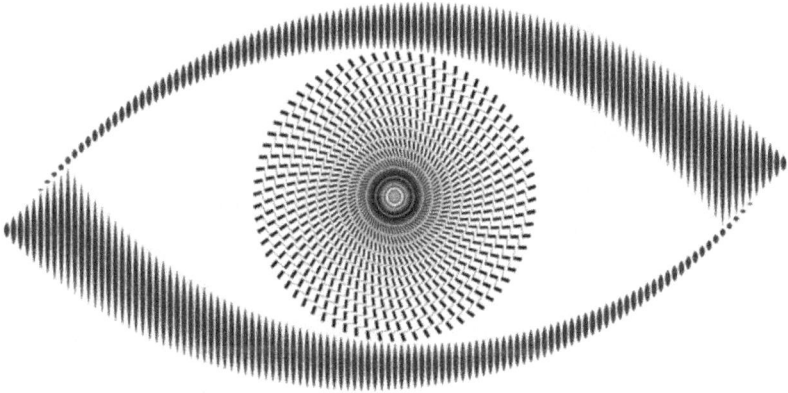

Poverty

Today you see your wallet empty, bank accounts,
empty, I guess this is poverty.
Waiting on that next pay, hoping for a miracle,
single parenting is difficult.
Grocery shopping is not fun, picking up items
adding each one, every single penny, I guess this is
poverty.

Can't complain or wreck your brain, look on the
bright side, all bills are paid you have your own ride.
Live in the moment, be grateful for all you have,
people are living without a mom and dad.
It doesn't matter if you're surviving through charity,
I guess this is poverty.

In life tables turn, so if things are down, know it's
bound to turn around. Embrace the lessons, soon
you'll see blessings. The light that's inside you
shines through, the cracks, the scars poverty bought
upon you.

Abundant in love and forgiveness, you're making
better choices, now you have clarity.
I guess this is poverty.
No, you overcame poverty!

Nature

Nature keeps me grounded, the breeze blowing
through trees, listening to waterfalls with water up
to my knees.
Such pureness helps me stress less, birds singing
and sending me messages. I enjoy being barefoot as
I walk along the beach, in the park, roots from the
earth enter my feet.

All chakras aligned, looking up at the sky, arms up
spread wide. An amazing stretch, trying to touch
the sun, I know that's farfetch.
Don't hurt to imagine, it's called manifestation,
levels at a high vibration.

No other place brings more peace than this
orchestrated universe that surrounds me.
Rain hitting my window pane, soothing is the
feeling I always gain.

Off to sleep I go, muscles relaxed from head to toe,
dreaming about all the lessons that help me grow.
This is what I call rest at its best and going with the
flow.

Snakes

Snakes, Snakes and more Snakes, time to clear my
space. Must protect my energy from the fakes.
Those who smile in your face but really deeply hate.
Harder when it's family, wearing a mask constantly,
so sad they're struggling, need to stop comparing.
We all have our own journey, some succeed more
slowly.
Self-reflect to get back on track, time to separate
from the pack.
Be a lone wolf, stand in your power, plant that seed,
bloom like a flower.

Snakes, Snakes and more Snakes, watch your step,
live in grace.
Always move at your own pace.
Shining brighter, flames stay lit to your fire, too hot
to handle, negative thoughts melt like wax on a
candle.
Good riddance snakes, hello faith.

Accident

It's rush hour traffic moving bumper to bumper,
things starting to pick up slowly.
BANG!! A crash, I was hit abruptly.

In shock, what was this guy thinking, did he not pay
attention, was he drinking?
Next day I can't move, the pain is excruciating, I
should go to the hospital or chiropractor,
anticipating.

I've got to work, got money to gain.
It's no way possible in all of this pain.

Appointment schedule, MRI reveals, the inevitable,
Spinal, soft tissue, cervical injuries, unimaginable.

Physical therapy is a must.
Don't know how to overcome it, to try is such a

bust.
Deep depression sets in.
How could this happen, all I want is to win.

Only to compete with myself, more prosperity, love
and wealth.
Healing process begins, not knowing it would be
such a transformation.
The power of grace healed me physically and
spiritually. I'm ready for a new journey, what's the
next destination?

Curtains Lifted

Time for the show to begin, a little nervous,
sweating, why am I second guessing.
I practiced a lot, the pain was real. I thought I had
enough time to heal.
Time for the show to begin, so intense, such a rush,
kinda like this feeling.

Everything spinning, just take it from the top, that's
it, from the beginning.
Time for the show to begin, yes everyone is
watching.
It's okay if you don't get praised.
People are toxic, for some it's just how they were
raised.

Time for the show to begin, you finally step in.
Bright lights, you're a star that shines from within.

Never forget it, you are gifted.
Wow! Amazing how my energy has shifted.

On to the next

Why is moving on so complicated.
We weren't even together in a committed
relationship.
I met someone who is more interested, he wants to
love my mind and body, he seems more dedicated.

This is what I pray for, now it's here, I have so
much fear.
My life in shambles, is it really meant to be, he is so
incredible.

It's a bit of an age difference, when in public, will
we be judged for our appearance.

Not my thoughts, just feels like what he's thinking.

So curious why he chose me, I know I'm a good
person, the question is, is that what he can see?
It's happening so fast, I'm trying to take my time,
and I want to avoid mistakes from my past.

He seems so put together, never sways, no matter
the weather.
This could be it, my forever.

Loving myself is top priority right now
So I'll just embrace the gesture and take a bow.

Baby girl

My baby girl I'm so proud of you.
The day you were born, only saw great things for
you.

I love all my kids but you really forced me to grow.
Want to always be your hero, to look up to as we
watch time go.

From age 4 you wanted to be a doctor, pediatrician.
I know you will succeed, feel it deeply, that's my
intuition.

You're so much like me, so much drive and
ambition. Graduating high school ahead of time, a
whole year early.
So focused on school, not boys, never being too
girly.

I love you just the way you are, that will never
change no matter how near or far.
You just shine bright superstar.

Stay engaged with the universe, even when things
sway.
Go within, trust the process, know it's navigating
you to success.

I'll be here for you always until the day I rest.
Even then I'll be guiding you from above so that
you always do your best.

No games

I don't have time for games, I'm so done with the
damage you cause to my brain.
How do you walk around in all that pain, carrying
such a burden would drive me insane?

Just make up your mind already, pick a side, pick a
side.
Don't seem like you can, acting like I'm your
woman then saying I'm a friend.

Giving mixed messages, incomplete sentences,
when will this cycle end?
Sick of you treating me like I did you wrong back
then.

I said I need space, it goes in one ear and out the
other.
I really want to fix this, at times its like, why bother?

Brave is what I need you to be, heal internally, trust
and you shall see.
All the things destined for you and me.

Until then I can't pretend to be your friend.
Let's just say goodbye for now, take care, the end.

Unconditional

It seems no matter how much I prove, my love for you is true.
You choose to sit in illusion and do the hurtful things you do.
When will you see I'm not the one who caused the pain which sits deep within you?

This is a nightmare, then again life is not fair.
How can I still miss you so much my dear.

Spirit is working with us on this.
Although we have free will, it's gonna be a hit or
miss.

Constant back and forward, words of resentment
mostly through text.
What do you want from me, what do you expect.

The reality is you didn't have my back.
I play it cool though, never react or disrespect.

It's that my love has always been unconditional,
pure, most of all fruitful.
I usually fear nothing, don't know what this
connection is, it must mean something.

Why else would we feel so much passion, every
time we're together always showing affection.
The days are numbered, I must decide, fight or
quit?

Regardless of what choice I make, I can't stop
thinking about your warm hugs and the chill my
body feels from your sensual kiss.

Divine Time

Live your life with no restrictions, so what! You
have little money, it's not a conviction.
You are the only one who limits your fun. Want a
vacation, lay out in the backyard, bathe in the sun.

Surround yourself with likeminded people,
exchange ideas, vibe in sequence.
Open your heart space let love in, dating without
sex is not a sin. Set boundaries, live up to your
expectations, never settle, have some patience.

Manifest your goals, believe and you will achieve. Even if you're not spiritual, most people know about Adam and Eve.

What's the new business you want to start or a job that sits in your heart.
It's your journey even if it's living on the streets. I believe you can come back from anything. Go within and seek.

Look for a sign, quiet your mind.
What's destined to be you shall find, all things are possible but only in divine time.

No worries

Worrying takes you off your path, life feels cold,
dark, like a window open at night, a chilling draft.
It's ok to close it, shut off your mind.
Stay focused on one day at a time.

Call up a friend, have a kick back, relax.
If you like the gym, exercise, take a selfie make sure
you flex.
It's so easy to lose yourself in worry, planning one
day to the next.
What's important is stopping to give thanks, take a
breath.

After having the chance to recharge, manifest your
new start. Open up that window, let all the fresh air
flow.
Notice the look on your face, abundance, what a
glow! No more worry yesterday is gone, time to let
it go.

Live for today

Live for today, be productive, ambitious and
continue to pray.
Live for today, it's a new day, yesterday is gone,
tomorrow is under way.
Live for today, stay stress free, let the negative
thoughts float out to sea.
Live for today, embrace the sun, lay on the beach,
take a walk or run.
Live for today, have no expectations, best things
come to those with patience.
Live for today, fulfill your wildest dreams, attend

events with the coolest themes.
Live for today, find happiness within yourself, fly
like a butterfly, take care of your overall health.
Live for today!

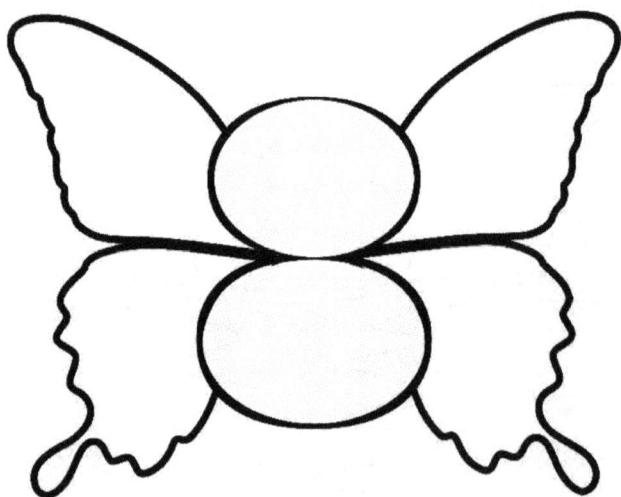

#8

Elevated each day, never letting negativity get in the way.
Infinite balance is on the horizon, use diligence, it's divine timing.
Goals are necessary, it pays off despite the contrary.
Highest potential required, the world relies on it, even if you get tired.
Time is fluid although you may feel stuck, when you see the number eight, ask your angels for help as you put in the work.

Empty

Hollow is the feeling inside.
Wanting to speak up, but too much pride.
Been on this roller coaster called life, such a scary
ride.
Could never be prepared for the next corner.
Closed eyes, heart beats faster.

Finally catch your breath, up next is the drop.
This is insane, did my heart just stop?

Time to get off this ride, start anew.
Endings always seem hard, much easier after a few.

If you didn't like the last ride, now you know
moving forward.
Whatever you do, don't become dormant.

At this point you have nothing to give, drained,
exhausted, questioning, "Should I live?" The answer
is yes, you are enough, uniquely blessed.

Feed that awesome soul, self-love, health, growth.
Now look at you, your feeling whole.

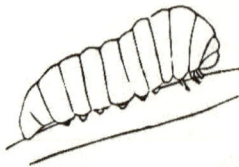

Butterfly

In this cocoon, so dark, hoping to see the light
soon. I get it, it's a life cycle, been here for a while.
As a caterpillar I feel so restricted, these changes
were not predicted.

A metamorphosis can be painful, only if you fight
it.
Trust the process, try to relax a bit.

The old body dies to form a new.
At this stage it's nothing more to do.

Stay in your protective shell.
All is bound to turnout well.

Nature is taking its course.
Your wings are developing, no need to force.

Now all the stages are complete.
Feeling renewed, never skipping a beat.

A gorgeous creature, happy tears I cry.
Time to spread your wings and fly high, my
precious little butterfly.

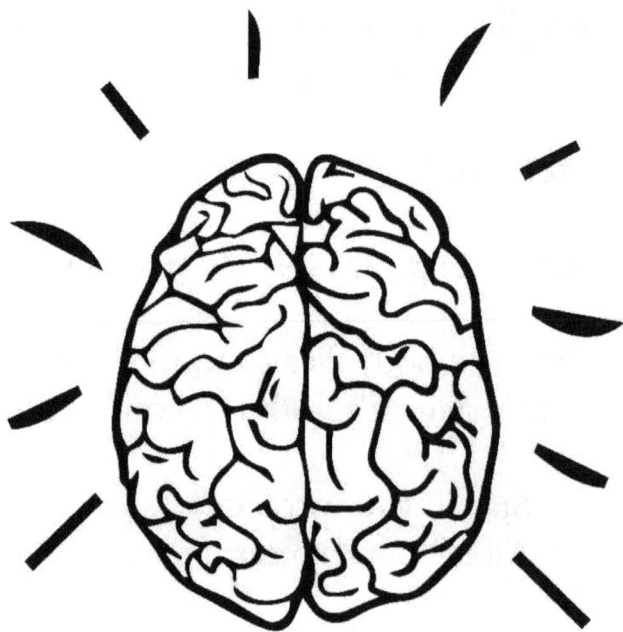

Trust self

There is no comparison to your inner being.
Always got your back, never fleeing.

The most trusted with your life. Not your friend,
family, husband, or wife.
They're not always right. You are an individual
uniquely divine.
The creator was strategic making you, definitely,
took his time.

So many times searching for answers in the wrong
places.
People wearing masks, not revealing faces.
Your intuition telling you this is not right.
Mind bottling, heart pumping an intense fight.
Believe your inner being when you see
synchronicities, there's no such thing as
coincidences.

Of Course you have free will, do what you like, each
time you ignore the signs it's a battle played with
your life, stay safe, trust the process and most of all
stay blessed.

Guarded heart

Tie a bow around my heart.
Cherish it like a gift, help me lower my guard.

To truly love, you must let it go, past pain doesn't
let you grow.
Healed people have a certain glow.

It's ok if you're not there yet, take time, get your
strength back, continued cycles are a fact.
I appreciate you for loving me, never doubt that.

My guarded heart is no longer.
You made it easy to love you, it made me stronger.

Insecure

Emotional security from an insecure person is like
flying solo.
Dead weight feeling heavy, how though, their heart
is hollow.

Time to let go, possibility of change is a no show.
All I really want is to grow.

It'll be nice to share my life.
Insecure men can't handle an independent wife.
The role expectation of society.
Men strong provider, women nurturer, quiet and
holy.

Don't make sense trying to fit in, be you, uniquely
divine, you will always win.
Not having faith is a known sin.

If you're not spiritual, at least try to be universal.
Connect with something higher than you, you're
really never alone, that's my truth.

ABOUT THE AUTHOR

Kiane Young is the CEO and Founder of Tranquil Conversations LLC. Virtual consultant business. She is from the small island Bermuda which is a very beautiful place to vacation, however the opportunities for growth are very limited. As a teen mom and survivor of abuse and dysfunctional environments she has experienced many challenges and has faced extremely difficult circumstances throughout her journey of life. Now, she is a mom of three and an entrepreneur that has over 10 years of experience consulting with individuals by helping them towards their desired goals through the beauty industry and in general life, she is ready to share her deepest thoughts and experiences with you. Kiane realizes that breaking through obstacles in your life is all based upon perception and has mastered the ability to navigate through some of the hardest lessons life could throw at a person. She has a top secret tool box, tools collected over the years, it is filled with tools specifically designed to fit your personal situation that will ultimately unlock the personal power within you. This book of poems is considered to be one of those tools. Kiane wants you to know that you are not alone on your journey and she is here for you to help you to break through barriers and fulfill your true purpose in life.

tranquilconversations.com

www.ingramcontent.com/pod-product-compliance
Lightning Source LLC
Chambersburg PA
CBHW022106020426
42335CB00012B/850